The Chime

The Chime

POEMS BY

Cort Day

Alice James Books

FARMINGTON, MAINE

Grateful acknowledgement is made to the editors of the journals in which these poems first appeared (sometimes in slightly different forms):

AGNI: "Elect Bastard Toadflax," "A Little Song About Negative Capability," "A Little Song About Plastic"
Boston Review: "Not a Cloud in the Sky," "Mouth"
Colorado Review: "Oceanid," "Red Adventure," "Reel Change," "Gris-Gris," "The Tare," "Axios," "Thistle Flower"
Fence: "Lung," "Zebra Grazes," "The Wrong Crowd"
Green Mountains Review: "Daylight Savings Time at Puerto del Sol"
Interim: "Red Mill," "Pleiades"
Pequod: "Tool & Die," "The Sunsuit of Aubergine"
Spinning Jenny: "Marsha in Constant Revision," "Antithesis," "Tiny Fable"
Verse: "Because Twilight, Isotropic & Permeable," "A Little Song About Darkness," "Throwback," "Skin"

"White, Ordinal" was first printed in Denver Quarterly.

Thanks to the MacDowell Colony, for a fellowship that provided time to work on these poems. My thanks to all of those whose friendship and acumen helped this book along, and including Richard Day, Forrest Gander, Matthea Harvey, Jane Mead, Peg Peoples, and Tessa Rumsey. Special thanks to Geoffrey Nutter for allowing me to farm in his field. Thank you Kate Egan.

Alice James Books gratefully acknowledges support from the University of Maine at Farmington and the National Endowment for the Arts.

Alice James Books are published by the Alice James Poetry Cooperative, Inc., an affiliate of the University of Maine at Farmington.

Alice James Books
238 Main Street
Farmington, Maine 04938

www.umf.maine.edu/~ajb

Library of Congress Cataloging-in-Publication Data
Day, Cort
    The Chime : poems / by Cort Day
      p.   cm.
ISBN 1–882295-29-3
I. Title.

PS3554.A9565 C67 2001
811'.6—dc21   00-062621

for my family

CONTENTS

I

II

III

IV

Instead of saying that oddness is the cause of odd numbers,
you will say that monad is the cause of them.

— PLATO, *Phaedo,*

Benjamin Jowett, translator

1

Not a Cloud in the Sky

Off to market. Not a cloud in the sky.
I'm hosting a flashover, right here in my head.
I am setting all the puppeteers to dancing.
And this time, there's no current in my chair.
In the work shed I'm making a dead civilization.
The fibers full of volts—my best suit.
In my dreams I run from tree to tree.
All the gods on this plain are capacitors.
I'm taking Aesop as my *nom de guerre*.
I am telling the story. I am full of light.

White, Ordinal

Displays a white surface a hush
grows out of. Installs white boxes,
white string, white logic, white keys.
Note that the old lists have been fused
in a new and stronger one. Reach inside,
a forest turns. Reach, you just might touch
your father's hand, your mother's face. As this
displays, the forest hardens. As this is white,
the forest turns, dangerous. So you turn
softly. You are holding "fields of phlox."

A Little Song About Plastic

Then the capital of fun stood glowing on the floor.
We ran inside it, full of hysterical plasma and rotating
to our favorite popsong, an electrical polka
about an increase in malignant tissue
in the suburbs. Right then, I spent my inheritance
on a basket of plums and followed the crowd to a field
where a funambulist had just been crucified
for poaching an egg. By then my voice was "a neutral,
highly ionized gas" involving the entire planet,
and then it was my turn, and I had nothing to say.

Thistle Flower

It begins with silence, a thistle flower
grown in someone's private lesson
and noticed there, and brought to your street,
to your door—resplendent node, thought
meant to assay you. From silence, the garment
of remembering. From the bones in the field,
the sound of trees. The deer get up
and go into the woods, remembering nothing.
My hand grazes your cheek. The garment
is willed to us. And the lesson begins.

Elect Bastard Toadflax

Elect bastard toadflax. It's the ancient healing
formula. The mathematics, located in the
nautilus, are so powerful they stop the sprite
from getting manic depressive. Elect, and get
aurora borealis piped into your family
reunion. Aunt Sophie's newfound radiance
will not fail to startle. A coherent, wave-like
syncopation will invest you, and you'll notice
a tiny application running inside everyone:
disposable, disposable, disposable, disposable.

Entropy Memoir

There's a leak in the think tank. A few loose experts float in and out.
They're all at least a thousand years old, and they can't stop muttering
about the end of the world. No one, it seems, can pinpoint the leak,
and these days the younger crowd likes to drive out there
after stopping at the Tastee-Freeze. The weather is different, blustery.
Once an entire mastodon floated by, once a fossilized pygmy village.
Parents used these occasions to talk to their children, some of whom
began having sexual dreams involving swans. Many who grew up
and left the area returned to find the town gone, except for the rain
and the voices of the experts, which had never been human at all.

Red Adventure

No time to waste, little cat's paw.
She was engaged in yards of blood, yards of cloth.
I was fully present, a red sail.
The surf had been emptied of ancestors.
Nothing to crawl out of. No scansion.
"All the way evil inside," says the poster.
No disharmony in the skyline.
Our gesture, a dulcimer.
I was the only botanist in the precinct.
I classified us as bone ash, then as lilies.

Ode to Vern

Things aren't so bad. The Apocalypse is sleeping.
It's got a stitch in its side, and there's a small tumor
growing on the back of your house. The tumor
reflects the gardens and trees, and right now Vern,
your neighbor, is mowing his lawn in it, upside down.
Tonight the tumor will cancel the lights in the sky
and report a flat, gelid void. Things don't look good, Vern.
If someone drops by to sit in your darkened living room
and talk about a "nervous feeling," open your eyes
as wide as you can, and blow your moonwhistle.

Dawn, Ordinal

Dawn arrives to excavate my dream. It's green again,
huge ponds of green to sleep inside. Green
cumulus, green church of inflecting light
deepening to trust the wills of children, gardens,
rusted lawn chairs to appear at wells of stillness—
this one full of rain, that one of song.
Light lays an edge against. These concave bodies
rise and fall in cages of memory, green,
kyrie eleison, I peel an orange
and wake its juice against her skin.

Pleiades

All night the Pleiades shone on my nipple.
Skull making investments in the sacristy.
Buy cormorant low. Sell cormorant high.
The docile have eaten their weight in gold.
I'm here to avenge: cormorant.
In my bird costume. The ocean's defunct.
The neoplasm comes in on a half-shell.
The seabirds arrive to "stir the blood."
Every portfolio has a tapeworm.
Outside this reticulum, I love myself.

Incubus

Ichor in the veins or nothing, to ass-fuck
a woman in a field of fireflies merely
because it's possible implies a fault
in the kiln, one large enough to admit
the fireflies, the lecherous gods, and me.
She trembles like a reed, I tremble, the gods
tremble like animals but can't remember why.
Why: ichor in the trees, fireflies in mindless
consciousness of field, the field a pleasure
synapse repeating *blood, clay, sky*.

Throwback

I only get ten minutes in this mask.
I rollick in the fisheries like a boy.
Happy among the dragnets and fish patties.
They say my brain's a real throwback.
I'm learning to juggle my addictions.
Today I let the blood out of a dog.
And now I know that something is innate.
The sand is fashioning a retort.
"There is no resemblance, no kingdom."
I sell you the words for nipple, for strawberry.

Tiny Fable

Darling, your infant's been whispering
into my Dictaphone again, and its tiny fable
scares me: it says the new Disposable Symphony
will repixelate all property as green or
"rain is money." Right now its voice is a lake
and a chemical, right now the voice is on fire.
It's reproducing the wood, phoneme
by phoneme, it's generating "dappled sunlight"
and "ideas of God" so quickly, there's no time
to drag the river for the missing—

Pastoral with Incubus

Whose regions—sickened, dispossessed—
grew silver in the gloaming, my own sweet incubus
speeding through strains celestial music
from zircon lakes and mountain-top fragments
left whole and shining. What was twilight
and passed-through glitters acutely
aware with incubus embedded, gleaming,
in light-shape fields, in rain ponds signifying
worlds held briefly in the throats of frogs.
You come back sweet, give way to nothing.

Rhizome Forest Waltz

I'm walking through the empty set, making guesses.
I guess: a documentary about the pleasure principle.
There's an ice storm in a town with one red lover.
There's a drop-dead forest that's perfectly accurate
and doesn't plan on being saved. Tomorrow, in the Spring,
I'll put on my softest suit, my moth suit, and go out looking
for my imaginary wife. She'll be here and there
among the mangroves and coral, and we'll both be amazed
at the living and dying getting done in our extremities,
at the rafts of sleeping children our breathing lets in.

//

Monad, a Deluxe Pastoral, Deepens and Unwinds

I.

When monad's volatile, I'm a firefly,
and you're a lake in white organza.
As monad renders, you pixilate,
and I'm a blood stain on a field of ice,
monitor me. Nights, monad's a lobe
of tiny fires we arrange to sleep inside:
the forest is programmed to self-sow. The rain
has left its feelings in our glade. We lay the wealth
on the ground at night. It deepened.
When your body left my body, a chime.

2.

When your body left my body, a chime.
The sun, vibrating imperceptibly,
causes monad to invest in chains
of waterfalls, green vitreous strands
I resonate inside. Investigate me.
I've been awarded a franchise.
When monad reaches point-of-sale,
you deepen briefly to a field of red
organza I enter as data encoded
in umbels and timbrels of wood thrush song.

3.

In umbels and timbrels of wood thrush song,
monad deepens. When sun activates
a song disorder to fructify the trees,
monad is the flowering system.
In green pools it deepens, terminal.
Terminal, it likes to destroy itself.
It suicides and flowers. It manifests
a fountain of blood in a hummingbird,
a body without *Arcturus* and *krill*.
Pieces of you missing, I darken.

4.

Pieces of you missing, I darken.
In inflorescence, in anemones,
I grow a mind: "my shadow in the sun"
is generating moneymen. Monad
suicides, they flower. Monad flowers,
they fructify. Inside a forest
of waterfalls and sugar trees that sound
like waterfalls, monad heals itself
by listening. If you touch hummingbirds,
moneymen appreciate. You touch them.

5.

Moneymen appreciate. You touch them.
Touch, and get a body without Arcturus
and krill. Feel, and unwind a sea aflower,
endlessly alight, and monad appreciates.
In a mind of water, a sunfish bites
my nipple. To organize itself.
In its scales, monad burns. An orange
thought, optical and burning, sunfish
shimmers reflexively in monad, then
as *laughing*, it rises to meet you.

///

Notes on the Basilisk

The lodestone is sapient and dreaming
of war. No, it's dreaming of a basilisk
asleep in a field of blood-wort and dreaming
of its mother—a moment of calm
in the life of a basilisk—and in the dream
a set of beautiful equations describes
a gamma-flower opening in language
a basilisk can't understand, but which
expresses perfectly the gamma in its head,
and gamma is what kills the basilisk.

Blue Garden and Rain

Lovers in the Rain is a toxic blue
garden filled with berries, and eating them
occurs throughout the fantasy
of the lovers going in and out of phase
inside it. It exhausts them—blue recursive
rain going in and out of phase and their own
instinctive motion to arrange themselves
on its surface. By now you are so thin,
there's a phosphorus-blue isotope
quivering like a sea inside you. Touch it.

The Sunsuit of Aubergine

He says, "There are no fish in the sound."
She says, "There is no sound," and it's true.
When she says, "We must put Aubergine into her sunsuit,"
it's understood: by tomorrow Aubergine
will be a teenager; the land is grown heavy with sleep;
Aubergine will rock gently back and forth
until the birdsong returns. The little islands stink
of wet wool. Later, as they make love, they try to imagine
Aubergine. And the moon rises, a tiny paring,
bringing almost no light at all.

Axios

Axios, my best disguise, burned while I was in it.
I was at the refinery, drunk and hated.
I came to in the floodplain. The plutocracy gleaming.
Above me, constellations: the Ladder in Flames,
the Virus, the Fly. My veins full of your poisoned wine.
Flotsam burned. Everywhere, you were dying;
I was killing you. I thought to flee into the billboard jungle,
then I fled. Imagine what I was: naked, millennia
streaming from my thighs. Where did I hide? Which organ,
which factory, which bird? Imagine, this is your body.

Mouth

I remember your face in the cigarette smoke
drifted and turned. I remember my baptism
at your mouth—labor of blackened tendons,
of hooks and eyes to drag a shape, the glutinous
tissues jumping to sound: it must be your heart
began as light as cork and dead to sound, then, sounding,
went out, down, dragging the face and its illusory
life. Some fossils leave a living coelacanth,
momentary residue, and though you'd disapprove,
inside my mouth your stone fish rise and sing.

Skin

Today's the day we privatized the water.
There's a parade at the site of the first vacuum.
We've tuned the ocean to an open frequency.
Pocket birds sing on floro-static lawns.
Optical children sleep in the trees.
Their bedtime stories pollinate the flowers.
The founder's gathering moss in the harbor.
The sentinel's giving head in the mint.
There's a lightning storm on the edge of my skin.
Inside you, a smell of chlorophyll and rain.

Lung

It's summer. Dad's polishing the chrome again.
He's just been fired from the razor factory.
Mom's out shopping for nougat at the mall.
There's been a small change in the pattern of the dog.
Not as frisky. Moves like a long narration.
Or separate pieces of a high, white sky.
There are surprising numbers of cats in the trees.
Dad doesn't notice. Mom thinks it's funny.
Years later she says, "We were never happy in that town."
She remembers not-I as "fireflies in the yard."

The Tare

He's in the intersection, talking to the victims,
perpetrators, witnesses, touching their elbows
that they might yield to him history's
one stable particle. He's the sound of bees,
he's a mountain of blood. All morning the rain
fell through his hands. O, they know he's lying,
he doesn't collect anything, but they comply,
amused at how alike they are, at how strange it is,
the floating feeling, the attendants attending,
the lights explaining, the truck backing up to

Elegy for Still Life

I'm using reflectometry to measure a cosmos
under a sheet. This one appears to weigh about
12 lbs. and still contains pieces of source code,
notably of a program enabling cats
to live happily in abandoned villages.
Such was your life, sonorous glyph. Outside,
the moon has shorted out, the Crab Nebula's
in tears. A girl keeps exploring a boxcar
and finding the body of a hanged man.
I sleep backward toward a face I can't transmute.

The Alewife's Dream

Evading sadness, her petticoat sky
dreams a dream in which she straddles
hour by hour the embolism
whose rough company she'd disown
but for cuttings grown by the orange window
in jars, orange because orange light
reposes like a beautiful alewife
on the blond and terrible marshes
where the horizon shines like a trumpet
and she gathers us up, shy and entire.

Night

There's nobody here to metabolize
the gift, no bright-eyed queen to whistle
Mozart to the jay. There's a loneliness
that can't arrange itself, that iterates
the only night of which it's capable—
breadcrumbs leading to blowjobs that go
nowhere, doorways feigning memory,
pine groves where the wind still stammers
about the child, the muslin sheets, the house,
the night that begs to dream of you.

Because Twilight, Isotropic & Permeable

Because twilight is permeable and remembers
to let a granular music come out of
the person you're fucking in the picture
window, it also comprehends the sackcloth
corpse leaning forward in your ribcage,
the language reacting on your tongue
to form the near field, the far field,
the beautiful face, eyes closed, floating
beside you in a lighted pane that twilight
constantly urges you to abandon.

Pièce de Resistance

No one can resist her impulse to drown.
It's sexy, the oceans inside her
conspiring to sustain the rhapsody.
Things fall. The skeptic leaves her side
a heretic, devout for having felt
her tug. Leaves fall inside the bishop's skull.
He can't sleep. She fucks carp to earn his light,
she fellates pike. The dogwood blooms.
An icecap's as inductive as his thought—
the whole of it awake and bright with worship.

A Poor Choice of Words in the Meadow

Volitionless Nature, why don't you call?
My bygones riff the clumsy trees.
I'll put down my jar a mile from here.
I'll inherit a necklace of holey dollars.
Here is a meadow. It is carbon.
Around it the stonemint grows and grows.
You are inside it, tiny iota.
And that is my hyena on your chain.
I hear your flute in the clanking grasses.
Your prayer burns on the end of my tongue.

Marsha in Constant Revision

The concubine is fragile. She, Marsha,
grows wild in desert highlands and indicates
for *succubus* and *cup of gold*. In movies
she's a blue howitzer sequence, the reason
men sweat to make a pile of stones equal the sun.
Turn up the sun, and she extrudes a fine dust called
"forlorn hope." The sound you hear is not weeping.
The stones are merely silent. Weeping will occur
after you and will come from the goddess,
Marsha, turning and turning in the blue water.

Red Mill

I'm writing a sonnet
about the difference between a dove
and a cyst. In general the dove
grows faster, the cyst more evenly.
Seen through the lens of the lingua franca,
both are blossoms in the thought of one for whom
"lay of the land" is part harmony, part porn.
The signage on the strip will testify. I'm in here
running spot checks, hoping to glimpse my sisters
when they come out of the red mill.

A Little Song About Darkness

The world of dew is the gleaming mask darkness
wears to narrate its arousal by submission.
Its physiognomy shines. Ibises shine,
ignorant of their enormous file size.
Ibises narrate the contingency of things
held in dawn light. There's never an ibis missing
because ibises are gnomons the light grows
inside itself to prevent forgetting. Darkness
grows inside the body of the noble savage,
who is pacing, pacing the shoreline in tears.

Argosy

My argosy leaves the harbor and falls.
Dawn, with its inane ventriloquism, comes up shy.
I'm headed toward a flat radar shadow.
I'm moaning in the brains of egrets and doves.
Each day the sun makes a syllable, a rebus.
Yep, the sun is a killer. It's full of oil.
And the moon totters. The moon is for subtraction.
It's reciting the lineage of mahogany.
I'm here to penalize the cosmology.
Rain drenches the trees, and it smells like money.

Academy of Science

The work's in progress. Bare winter trees
are metallurgy in a cube of light
so dense its energy deracinates
antipodes. Here is calm and purpose.
Organelles divide themselves beneath the weight.
The pixels burn. Delicate surgeons
inflect the orgy with markers and dyes
and hope to watch the demiurge
tell Helen to open her lovely thighs
to bring the gods and burn the ships of reason.

Bestiary of Ramona

"Admire me I am a violet," I keep
telling you, secretly hoping the snow
will fall and make me less anonymous.
It won't, and tonight a negative forest
grows beneath the trees, grows flat on the ground,
and everything above it is a forest
word in which it's possible to hear the Elk,
the Fawn, the Fox, the Bear
walk out of your hands to drink
from the falling pool, the moon-blind water.

Desert Oblique

A convection of voices. A drum.
I mime their desert in my foxhole.
Me with my voltage, my electrical grid.
Now: rain to scrub the village clean.
Sun to make the voices diverge and swell.
White bedclothes hang undulant in song.
The keeper a tree of bleached bone.
The horizon a book of voices of bone.
Now: a litter of flowers. The people are dancing.
Dancing and swirling at the ecstasy pulpit.

Epithalamium: Swans for Geoffrey

When in the Great Lawn it was time to forsake yourselves,
the bride was a flock of sparrows. So Geoff went a little apart
and made a poem for Zyrafete, protector of virgins,
describing the happiness of sparrows. Zyrafete heard,
and into the Great Lawn in radiance Maria bore such tidings
that even as a bee in the thalamus of a flower I tasted
the green fire being engendered there, and Geoff's word
rooted itself and grew strong, and held inside itself worlds,
and figs and pomegranates for Maria the Sylph of Waters,
and swans for Geoffrey, the Master with the Mountainlike Clouds.

IV

The Wrong Crowd

To feel good is prime, though perhaps I ought not
perform the monkey-jacket dance, that slow and vulgar
ballet of defloration, that bit of hothouse
frippery. It's sure to attract the wrong crowd—
Jezebel singers, Jezebels, float critics, anglers,
harmony babies, atmosphere ranchers, runts—
who don't care whether the mountain's detached
from its shadow, the honeybee from its chain,
who'd be more than happy to watch the avatar,
surrounded by addicts, begin his hemorrhage.

Happy Hour

We saturated that elegy years ago,
pegged its tunings into a curse
no one could hear, then stood upwind
for the explosion. What's left to debunk?
The gods are hiding in the bamboo
or mingling with tourists at the milk bar,
hoping to be spared. The frigate with the microscopes
carries the plague. A knight-errant's mixing drinks
to keep us simple and in love, simple and in love
with him and his foolish tales of Apollo.

Zebra Grazes

Zebra is a waveform, grazing in organic.
Then it gets a premonition or decays.
If premonition, we witness it in flight,
proving it hates to lose. If lion gets
released, with premonition, zebra loses.
Invest in lion and never wake up
in zebra's bleeding skin. Invest in zebra
and balance a waveform. Why invent disorder?
At night I crawl among the sleeping herds
and redden them slightly with my apple.

Oceanid

Long have I loved you, oceanid.
The bejewelled ochlocracy inscribes your name.
Your tortive logic makes me quiver.
I pin currencies to you. They rise and fall.
You sleep in a fairy-ring in the corner of my room.
You sing in your sleep when a schooner rounds the horn.
I look until lumens gutter on the sill.
We step in the traps the rain sets, one by one.
When I'm a porpoise, you're getting horny.
In the morning you're a wolf, and I'm a gar.

Reel Change

She was a blue panel of self-delight.
Deep aqueous fjords, anemone and sponge.
I was peddling thin mints from an icicle cage.
In the split-second reel change the pregnancy took.
All my coins falling by the early water.
The immense chords all iron, all salt.
No cynicism in the faces of the waves.
No science when the unheard-of voice begins.
The sky was a libertine. She was a sculptor.
We believed. Around us the blood began to knock.

Recombinant Poem on the Birth of a Child

"Lens and blown seed" was the zygote.
River-blood on a meadow.
Where the face in its caul grew.
"Innocent" meaning "accident," meaning
the face. Riparian, marine, held.
In her arms. In the ocean-light
of the hospital room, a cry, a small skin
without analog, a disorder innocent
of our repairing shadow
became *amen said looking backward,* then—

Strand

The doctor insists I repeat "I'm a dead horse"
to the mirror, so I repeat, although it seems likely
I'm a microscope or photo-cell asking
if pelicans might flourish out of mind,
or if my virtue activates their lives. Figure I
shows how motions in my skull account
for minute changes in the color of the sea.
That child has my mother's eyes. On the strand,
Venus makes her way ashore through mines
I planted to avoid these circumstances.

A Little Song About Negative Capability

With: in the melting, I was so moved,
I composed: the chunks of ice the moon
lit paused then rushed the falls, their dull boom
going through pure weight, resonating fact:
she composed there out-of-faith in gleaming
wilderness: we touched the long, white cells
of memory: the ice composed from flaws
distorted forms that accelerating past
gave back reflected ice-bright cradles
to resist the heart-stopped forest: love.

Antithesis

The loosed hounds course inward to the zero
landscape, zero forest, sun-hot zephyr,
and are gone. The smell is gone, the format.
The neatly woven strands, the imagined
half-living quantum cat have lost their pulse.
Now what bread will be brought to the table?
Out of the gross data, what particle
will thirst irritate to consciousness of light?
There is a void more ravening than the sea.
Who sits there? What taste in the mouth of the god?

Caesar in the Lake

Caesar goes in his jolly-boat alone.
He's already wearing his organic clothes,
his archaic smile. His mind's a koan:
inside the floating-point error this one made.
He can't concentrate. The peace and quiet
have worn holes the size of landmines in his head,
through which he feels the theme park quiver and shine.
He dozes. His mouth full of honeycomb.
He sings in his dream, a sound almost like blood,
like blood's apology, like no blood at all.

Daylight Savings Time at Puerto del Sol

Like everything, the sun's a monotype.
It spreads its red reaction through the trees.
The birds here survive by feigning extinction.
The chemical colors are a dead giveaway.
I've used up my share of the "deep water complex."
I'm grilling sun-steaks with my friend Janine.
The war channel keeps us attuned to the war.
Janine has the world's most expensive shoulders.
Tonight the moon will rise from her forebrain.
On the final planet we are makeshift, gorgeous.

Tool & Die

Tool & Die was the Lord's purpose.
With it he dug his furrow, sowed his seed.
Inside Tool & Die love blazed in a knot,
a coal. It was the clicking data string.
And since we've mapped the structure of *fern*
and *dung beetle*, it's evident the garden
grew from one bulb, with Tool & Die resident
and tactile: touch one bloom and the whole crone
flinches. On a bright day it's orchestral,
birth and fornication saying *touch me, sleep.*

Survey of Lit

I'm taking my kaleidoscope to the zoo.
I want to look at the penguins.
I'm going disguised as a waterfall
so it will feel as if one idea
is interviewing another idea.
I hope to trace the history of envy
to a bar in downtown Des Moines, then outward
so schoolchildren might see evidence
of the rolls of fat on the President's neck
in the methane ice-fields of Pluto.

Gris-Gris

The millwright polished a pebble and left.
I clutch my gris-gris and prepare for coherence.
Naturally, my teepee is made of plywood.
An alp floats by in a red satin suit-dress.
An ocean passes through a hummingbird's throat.
The ground thrush does not, officially, reflect the sky.
Look in the mirror: it's a close shave.
My friend Julie has a great summer job.
She herds a million buffalo into a temple.
I turn off the light and pray for reclosure.

N O T E S

The phrase "my shadow in the sun" is from Shakespeare's *Richard III*, Act I, scene i, line 26.

Lovers in the Rain is the title of a painting by Sharon Bental.

Axios is the name of a Greek river deity.

"The world of dew" is from a haiku of Issa, translated by Robert Hass.

"Admire me I am a violet" is from John Keats' letter to John Hamilton Reynolds, February 3, 1818.

"Desert Oblique" honors a performance by the late Dr. Nusrat Fateh Ali Khan.

The "half-living quantum cat" is Schrödinger's Cat, a postulate of the physicist Erwin Schrödinger.

Recent Titles from Alice James Books

ALICE JAMES BOOKS has been publishing exclusively poetry since 1973. One of the few presses in the country that is run collectively, the cooperative selects manuscripts for publication through both regional and national annual competitions. New authors become active members of the cooperative, participating in the editorial decisions of the press. The press, which places an emphasis on publishing women poets, was named for Alice James, sister of William and Henry, whose gift for writing was ignored and whose fine journal did not appear in print until after her death.

TYPESET AND DESIGNED BY MIKE BURTON

PRINTING BY THOMSON-SHORE